# Life
# Love
# God
# ...And All The Other Bullshyt

A Book By: Seleta Harvey

Copyright © 2017 by Seleta Harvey

All rights reserved.

This book or any portion thereof may not be reproduced or used in any manner whatsoever without the express written permission of the publisher except for the use of brief quotations in a book review.

Printed in the United States of America

First Printing, 2017

ISBN: 978-1-5356-0648-6

*Dedication*

THIS BOOK IS DEDICATED TO those who found the strength within them and used their craft for the betterment of others. To inspire them to seek out their greatest assets in order to help fuel others in fully believing in themselves, and to show how life can truly be from a different perspective. To those other individuals in my life that have helped transform me as well as my work, in order to help and heal others, I thank and love you all unconditionally. To my mom and dad —you guys have always believed in me from day one and always supported me in every endeavor.
#LiveLifePositive

In Loving Memory of
Rabbi Jehu A. Crowdy, Jr. GFA
"I will always meet you in the air."

# Contents

Chapter 1: Life ...................................................... 1

Chapter 2: Love ...................................................44

Chapter 3: God ...................................................64

Chapter 4: And All The Other Bullshyt........................89

# Life

"Even in quietness and stillness there is a certain strength and power that cannot be measured or even understood."

"Greatness is not determined by outward appearance but by attitude, character, and, ultimately, purity of heart."

"You should always strive to create a better version of yourself."

"When people start believing their own lies, they knowingly forget which mask to take off."

"Always be kind to those close to you because kindness is one of the reasons they are still there."

"Sometimes the smallest and simplest gesture can have an everlasting effect on the human psyche."

"You have no room to judge me unless you are living in my body and experiencing my pain."

"There is a difference between walking the path and standing on the side viewing the path."

"Make your own renovations within before seeking out another bodily space to occupy."

"Taking someone for granted is like pouring water onto your head and feeling a sting seep into a small cut you didn't know you had." "Never give someone your best when they have intentions of giving you their worst."

"If people were more consistent with their thinking and feeling, there wouldn't be so much internal conflict. Consistency is key!"

"Sometimes some people need to be kept at arm's length to keep them from damaging a good person."

"A man should never give a woman reason to be jealous."

"Those who are willing and able to listen are capable of opening their hearts."

"Sometimes the best lesson is learned by watching other people's actions."

"Chances are precious opportunities to get it right."

"To be truly free you must let go of all idealistic creations."

"Prepare every day to meet your new self tomorrow."

"No one gains from chasing or being chased…why not just meet in the middle and be equals?"

"All the qualities that you seek within yourself do exist in another body… find thyself to know thyself."

"If you can be truthful and genuine to yourself then you have the ability to be truthful and genuine to others."

"When life throws things at you, it is up to you what you want to catch and what to let miss you."

"It's not living that matters but living rightly."

"Your true character is defined not by your words but by your actions."

"There is so much that is gained when you fall on your knees and pray."

"What you don't deal with in your conscious mind will wreak havoc in your unconscious mind."

"Never perceive things with your eyes; always use your heart."

"There is something wrapped within us that is waiting for us to discover it."

"Use your own common sense to know when something is for you and when it is against you."

"My life consists of interesting characters…good thing I am an adventurous type."

"I am not looking for perfection because it doesn't exist."

"Life will offer many things, but it's your choice what to do with those picks."

"It doesn't cost you anything to be a positive influence in someone's life."

"Only you can define what type of person you want to be. The first step is making the choice."

"If you can't find the good in any situation then you must turn around and look within yourself."

"People must understand that common sense is critical in this thing we call life."

"Always strive to find the good in people because you don't know what type of Hell they had to go through to reach this point in life."

"There is always going to be something in life that just eludes you. You contemplate, dissect, analyze, but can never totally figure it out."

"Of all the things in life, love eludes me every time."

"Some people fail to see the light in the clouds, the wrinkle in the water, the tear in the drop, and the aroma in the flowers."

"There are some things in life we are not going to understand, and people will not always 'get it.' The important thing to remember is to keep on loving life and loving people, because that is a universal truth that everyone comprehends."

"Everything that you need to understand about your life is already in front of you."

"Sometimes we have an internal sadness in life that no one knows, and God is the only one that can heal it completely."

"Some fail to realize you will receive karma whether you did good or bad."

"Sometimes life will hand you things but you have to decide what is going to be for you."

"Some gifts that are received will not always be wrapped up and presented to you in the way you want."

"Whatever you give in this life and to others, make sure it is a gift and not a curse."

"What is felt lasts longer than what is seen with the eyes in life."

"If you're cut from a different cloth, then you should be careful about the people you touch. You don't want a stain that will never come out."

"If something is eluding you, it means that you are not ready to receive it."

"There must be a realization of your character before you can understand and define what you are."

"Being able to inspire others not only speaks volumes about your character but also shows that the Creator blessed you in another form."

"Sometimes the things that we say don't match up with the things that we are. Good or bad, be consistent."

"Negative things happen day in and day out. Even though they happens, never forget to see the beautiful and positive side of things. A spoonful of positivity in your life is good for your mind and soul."

"Toxic people will show you exactly who they are and what they are about. Make it your business to remove them from your life so they do not poison the good people in your life."

"Life shows us the most beautiful and the ugliest things we can imagine. However, when one ugly thing shows its face, do not focus on it; instead, pull out that one beautiful thing. Sometimes flipping the coin makes all the difference."

"A gut feeling is when your stomach tells you something is either right or wrong and travels along that string to your heart and your heart has a conversation with your brain. If one of them is 'out of order'…pray about it."

"Life has a funny way of showing you things you don't want to see and things you need to see."

"Life has a natural way of showing you…who you really are."

"Where there is room for error, there is also room for the process of growth to start."

"You final destination in life is not determined by the physical but is a mental perception of where your soul and spirit should lie."

"Sometimes in life you have to cut out the negative weeds in your garden in order for the growth process to flourish."

"Sometimes the things you want in life are out of reach for a reason."

"When someone doesn't require a lot of things, it means they have been blessed in more ways than one."

"The greatest challenge in life is not finding yourself but allowing your inner man and outer man to become one in peace and love."

"Tragedies are going to happen in life and there is no way to avoid them. However, it is what you learn from them that matters. It can change you from the person you are now to the person you are transforming into if you stay on the positive side. The only thing that can stop you is you. Don't allow yourself to get in your own way, because that's a tragedy."

"People are not always going to understand the level you are on. Those who are willing to learn will either grip the side of the ladder and step up to get higher or step down because of fear. Fear will keep you at the bottom and that's not where you are destined to be."

"Wherever you are lacking in your life, make it your business to do better. Do it for yourself to make you a better person inside and outside."

"Even though life may throw some stuff at you, people may mistreat you at times, and things may not always make sense, you must remember your path is specifically designed for you, and no one else can fit the shoes you need to walk it."

"Always cherish the small and happy moments that happen in life, because when things get hard it is going to be those simply precious moments that can take you to a serene place in your mind."

"Everything that happens in your life, directly or indirectly, does not always require a verbal response. Sometimes you have to visually see it, get the lesson and the message, and process it in your mind. Only then should you say afterwards, 'I learned something.'"

"Sometimes it takes something in our lives burning in order for something new to arise out of the ashes. So when you rise out of the ashes, you won't remember the pain but you will remember the experience."

"In order to get your horizon to that unlimited location, you must first be willing to think thoughts never conceived before."

"Sometimes the things that you need in this life will not just creep up on you but will smack you hard in the face so you do not question whether it was real or not."

"Treasure what you have now, love the people who are a part of your life, march to your own beat, live as you see fit, and see the beauty around you, because nothing lasts forever!"

"It takes a certain level of maturity to recognize your faults and make the changes, it takes courage to apologize to those you have hurt in some way, and it takes strength and trust to let someone in who only wants the best for you."

"When life starts to get a little weird and too serious at times, the best medicine is to go swing on a swing."

"When you come across good and genuine people, your first instinct should be to keep them around and not discard them. We cannot afford to mistreat, use, take advantage of, or throw away anyone, because at some point in your life you are going to need them."

"There are some things that you realize about yourself, and you should never have a problem being honest with yourself. You can love and care with such an intensity that some can't understand; it doesn't matter if you are a friend or something else. It comes from a very genuine place and it shows that you are cut from a different cloth."

"The things that you want the most in life do not come in the ideal format. You always have to use your peripheral vision to get the bigger image. There is always something more that is required, but it is ultimately up to you decide what the 'more' is and how to apply it in life."

"Never push someone away who genuinely cares for you, because you never know if they were sent to be a blessing in your life. We do not have the authority to throw anyone away."

"You and I may not have riches, but we are richly blessed on many levels; you and I may not have everything we want, but we have exactly what we need; you and I appreciate nice things, but they do not define the individual inside that we are; you and I have the love of many, but we only want the love of that one person. We are all a work in progress, so take us as we are or simply watch us walk away. Too many good women slip away because one was too scared or couldn't handle how real they were."

"Always seek to find the beauty in everyone that you meet, but some eventually show their ugly side and then you forget why you found them to be beautiful in the first place."

"You can always see the truth in the way you smile."

"Coming full circle happens when you have an experience that affects every aspect of your life. You then recognize and associate yourself with the emotions you are feeling, process the information, and formulate a conclusion that teaches you a valuable lesson."

"If you loosen the grip you have on reality from time to time then you will understand life a little better."

"The strength of your words relies on the strength of your character."

"Life is like falling snowflakes: each part is shaped uniquely and falls into place at different rates, but it is all determined by the Source."

"Seek the ways of understanding and learning about yourself and you will be surprised at what you discover."

"If we knew all the answers to life then we wouldn't have any questions to ask."

"Harsh words and actions can crush an innocent soul."

"What you see and feel should correspond with that you think."

"With deep introspection you discover the real you and everything that you are capable of doing."

"Discovering what your true Achilles heel is shows how determined and committed you are to being a better person."

"Everything that can be understood is not meant for you to understand it because it requires a higher level of consciousness."

"One of the things certain in life is that there will always be people that will hurt and disappoint you, but it's up to you to determine which ones are genuinely worth it."

"Never hesitate or be slow to accept good people in your life."

"Being a dynamic spirit means the learning process is still taking place in every aspect of your life. Embrace the good, get rid of the bad, and live as you see fit."

"Life is a comedian and we are the audience."

"Know the difference between love that is going to enhance your quality of life and love that can be destructive and volatile."

"Life is not supposed to be perfect. It's supposed to teach you perfect lessons so you can live better."

"There is a great understanding that is gained when you begin to fall."

"There are certain things we are built to understand and other things that are supposed to be felt out."

"Some things cannot be measured by length of time but by how much endurance you possess to stick it out until the end."

"You never know your true strength until you've been pushed."

"You have to allow things to take their natural course in order to understand the process."

"Always paint from your soul and leave what you feel on the canvas of life."

"Learn to appreciate the value of time and patience."

"A good person will only take so much and allow so much until they are pushed."

"There are those things that are worth it. It is up to you to decide what those things are."

"You can't make someone appreciate you if they are not willing to receive you just the way you are."

"Speaking positively in your life puts more air in your body so you can live."

"Find the beauty in the pain and the lesson in the sorrow."

"I'd rather be someone's sweet reminder than a painful flashback."

"A mental connection is more real than actual words."

"Some things are better understood when your vision is blocked and you have to use your ability to feel."

"If you can't find a reason to live more, then create the reason to live on."

"Heartache is the best teacher for the first step in being honest with yourself."

"Most battles do not have to be fought with aggression and an attitude. Silence is the best weapon against volatile action."

"Areas in your life may have a period, comma, question mark, or exclamation point. It solely depends on your perspective."

"It takes one lie to destroy that one natural mental connection."

"You are not qualified to box with my spirit."

"If someone fails to appreciate your time, then no longer give it."

"Once you find that spark that illuminates your life, hold on to it and never let go."

"The path will never be easy. Every challenge must be faced with courage and grace, but have the mindset to seek more from yourself so you can inspire someone else."

"You cannot change that which you contiunously ignore."

"Life can be everything you want and nothing you ever expected. All you have to do is roll the dice."

"It is better to know nothing and be open to learn everything."

"There is a reason behind your happiness that some cannot fathom or comprehend. The only truth you will see is in a smile."

"To seek the truth and find the peace within you must go beyond the surface of yourself."

"In order to acquire things in life, you must first be qualified to begin."

"When you begin to treat people in a negative way, it is time to check your own inner wiring and fix what is broken."

"When you struggle with the truth it means you are out of the practice of telling it."

"Being happy shouldn't require much thought or action; just let it be natural and simple…that's all you really need."

"Some stand at the shore watching the ocean, and others run to the ocean and dive in. Why? Because that is where opportunity and endless possibilities lie."

"If you understood the beginning then you shouldn't be at the end still asking questions."

"It is easy to tell when you meet people with good intentions and those with bad intentions."

"If you always learn stuff the hard way, you never appreciate something when it is simple."

"A good person with a good heart is a rarity that only few ever encounter."

"You can understand something better when it falls apart in your hands."

"True power is knowing another person's weakness and not exposing it for others to see."

"Not everyone is qualified to step into the ring and go toe to toe and box with you mentally, spiritually, emotionally, and metaphysically."

"Not everyone is fit to dress in the clothes that you wear, and you must take it upon yourself to find what fits you best. Only you can determine that and no one else!"

"Sometimes the best type of healing you need is the medication of your mind."

"Base your character off of how you would want to be treated."

"Never disregard your feelings; they are what make you human."

"Respect yourself enough to know what is good and bad for you."

"Remember, the lessons you learn in life will be the same, but the teachers will always be different."

"I'd rather be my own hero than be my own villain."

"When someone provides you with a reason to let them go, by all means, understand it and set them free."

"Find new meaning and new life in everything that you do."

"Your journey has instructions that only you can read."

"If you have too many excuses, that means you're letting your ego and pride speak for you."

"Ego and your spirit cannot live in the same dwelling."

"Love yourself to know when ego and pride is murdering the relationship that took time to build."

"Want to live a more fulfilling life? Evict ego and pride from your soul."

"When you finally meet someone just as real as you are, don't run and hide. Embrace it and love it because it was in your path for a reason."

"Speaking prolifically and sophisticatedly will bring a positive energy that will transport you to another plane of existence."

"If you cannot communicate properly, then your words fall on deaf ears and actions become static motions."

"People have the power to inspire you to do some wonderful things, as well as the dumbest things known to man. Tap into your higher consciousness and see things as they should be."

"A smart person will learn from their mistakes and not repeat them, but a fool will continuously make the same mistake, thinking that they missed something."

"Sometimes it is necessary to sit quietly with your eyes closed so you can focus better with your other eye. Everything you weren't able to see before you will begin to see clearly."

"The first step in being good to yourself is treating others well, no matter what the situation is."

"You must release the ego and pride in order to fall into the arms of humility completely."

"Sometimes you have to lose everything in order to gain it all back."

"The 'what if' thoughts lead to more uncertainty in your conscious mind and to unanswerable questions in your subconscious. The 'what is' thoughts rely on the already known facts and absolute truth. The 'what if' thoughts leave you in the shadows and the 'what is' thoughts direct you toward the light."

"Feeding your spirit is doing what is right and not what is easy, and feeling more deeply so it reverberates in the halls of your soul."

"If the individuals currently in your life are not inspiring you to be better and do better, then it's time to demote."

"Everyone has faults, but the smart ones learn how to fill and repair them in order to build a bridge over them to get to that next plane in life."

"The things in life are better experienced without all the verbal carnage that surrounds them."

"When you wake up with a new determination, that means God has put more push in you to direct you clearly to your purpose."

"Find your purpose…enhance your life!"

"In order to do new things in your life, certain things need to be sacrificed to make room for what God has for you."

"There is more to life than what you see with your two eyes: what you ultimately feel in your heart, soul, and spirit."

"If you have to struggle with a decision that is based on good intentions and love, then it's obvious you are not receptive to the possibilities."

"Happiness is the trigger that sets more good deeds into motion."

"Some people are closer to the edge of a breakthrough than they realize."

"The only competition you have is not allowing your 'old self' to catch up to your 'new self.' Elimination of your 'old self' in this race makes your 'new self' better."

"If you shine the angles of your sharp heart to the one most deserving then you allow that person to make it smooth and touchable."

"In a world that wants you to have a degree or specialize in something worthwhile, your main focus should be a degree in forgiving yourself; specialize in communication and get a masters from the Master of love."

"To be comfortable in the midst of your silence allows you to see and hear your inner and outer surroundings."

"Your inner man is able to reach beyond your own consciousness, a place your outer man doesn't have access to."

"Everything you touch, everything you say, and everything you feel should have nothing but positivity in it, because it definitely rubs off on people in an extraordinary way."

"We are forever learning how much patience, forgiveness, understanding, and trust really go hand in hand."

"Life is interesting in itself, but people make it more hilarious than you and I could ever imagine."

"The things that are meant to shake you up are also those things that are meant to inspire you to go beyond the surface and reach deeper into yourself."

"Sometimes it takes hurt, heartache, and disappointment to really invoke the gifts that God has for you. For in that struggle you realize your greatest aspect is the potential you have yet to tap into."

"The greatest challenge you will ever face is meeting your opposite and having them stare back at you."

"God grants us the opportunity to see what our puzzle of life looks like. God provides us with hints as to what puzzle pieces fit perfectly and also gives us freewill to see what pieces do not fit, whether they are people, places, or things. God knows the precise moment and time when a piece you are trying to fit does not belong on your puzzle. It is up to you to use what common sense God has given you to see what is for you and what is not. Stop trying to force a piece that does not belong or it will hinder the potential that you have now, which could ultimately affect your future."

"Meeting different people allows you the opportunity to gain something useful to better yourself. Every human encounter can make you stronger, wiser, and kinder."

"Your only mission in life is to grow into the individual you are meant to be, not what others want you to be."

"You have no room for unhealthy people in your life, for they will make you sick and deplete your life force."

"Have enough faith and trust in yourself to understand, visualize, and internalize all the potential that is wrapped inside. Everything will be revealed layer by layer…just embrace the process."

"When people are not able to digest the absolute truth that is given, it means that they have built up a tolerance against it and would rather have negative anomalies in their system."

"Ego and pride will kill so much if you allow them and don't humble yourself. If you don't humble yourself God certainly will."

"Actions of loyalty are different from the words of loyalty. One will be more true than the other."

"You discover exactly what you have built up inside when trouble comes walking, talking, and knocking in your direction."

"The most abstract thing about life is you never know what angle you are looking at and how to approach it effectively."

"When you start using people and not things, you've already kindled the fire that will eventually burn the bridge."

"Certain behaviors are expected from children, but when they transfer over to adulthood then you end up becoming the plaything."

"Some of the things in life can be solved if you added silence into the equation."

"There is healing when you right the wrongs in your own world."

"The best position to be in life is where you are open and receptive to the good things that surround you."

"You will never be able to comprehend something if you keep letting fear be a doorstopper and not allow the door of your mind to swing open."

"Stop running from something that is meant to enhance your quality of life."

"Running to something familiar will never change you. Only by walking away securely will it you change."

"The ones who are close to you will hurt you unintentionally, unknowingly, and unbelievably in a number of ways. It will get to the point that you will walk away not because you love them any less or want to inflict pain but because you love yourself more."

"Being able to admit that you were wrong or had some wrongdoings means you silence your ego and pride to the point where humility in you has taken over."

"You are only doomed in this life if you fail to recognize the change surrounding you."

"If some things seem out of focus, it just means you need to pay attention to what is going on inside you and prioritize your life on the outside. No amount of 'head shaking' is going to straighten or clear your focus."

"Always be thankful for the positive and small occurrences that happen to you, because it shows that you are paying attention, and when the big positive occurrences happen, you will have enough sense to embrace them humbly and openly."

"Some people are content with remaining on 'pause' or continuously hitting 'rewind' to the past because it is familiar. However, those who hit 'play' are the ones who are not afraid of the unknown and know how to embrace the positive change coming in the next scene."

"Where your heart wants to go ego and pride cannot follow."

"Some people's level of stupidity and ignorance is so disgustingly on another plane of existence that if you think about going there the toxicity of the acid will melt you away."

"Even the most understanding person can be misunderstood by some, but not by all."

"Adapting to unnecessary bullshyt is idiocy, but adapting to positive change is genius."

"The desire and passion for an intellectual connection should be stronger than that for an intimate connection."

"The greatest challenge we face as humans without unlimited conscious abilities is not just forgiving ourselves but forgiving ourselves for the ultimate hurt toward a genuine spirit."

"Life begins when you truly accept and digest who you are and who you belong to."

"You can never truly own anyone in this world."

"If you do the right thing, you will live longer."

"When someone touches your heart there is another level to missing their presence."

"Living a life of authenticity will naturally bring positivity in your direction, but living a life of false notions will bring opposition and chaos."

"Living a life of fear stumps your spiritual growth process."

"Nothing will bring you more satisfaction than the peace you find within yourself."

"Everything that you are should be consistent with what was taught to you in the inside."

"There comes a time when words will fail, but the actions of your heart will prevail if you show them."

"Your knowledge is the only truth you have until you seek to have a higher understanding and become fully aware."

"Open your eyes to what you see and look beyond for what is truly meant to be."

"The greatest understanding that you know is when you discover the truth from within."

"Within every person lies the heart of goodness. You have the choice of allowing that to come forth or hiding it for no one to ever experience."

"Knowing where home is and feeling where home is is something only your soul can tell you. Be smart enough to pay attention."

"Understanding something well enough doesn't make you an expert on it unless you had to learn the lesson more than once."

"'Home' is more than a place to rest your head; it's a place where your soul has finally found a peaceful dwelling."

"You will never know the outcome of the story if you are too scared to turn the page."

"The challenges of life will show either who you are meant to be or who you are not."

"When you find your reason/purpose, sometimes the only thing you can do is smile."

"Remember, your soul is older and wiser than logic."

"Never condemn someone who takes a 'time out' in order to gain balance within them."

"In the complexity of your problem there lies a simple solution. You only need to recognize the truth from the beginning."

"Exposure to the positive things will be reflected in you if you choose to embrace what they truly are."

"When you are in the midst of your blessing, act accordingly and accept it as it is."

"Never stop trying to find the God in you. You're never a failure when you are seeking the truth in yourself."

"The only way to describe the best and worst parts of life is by living it as you see fit."

"You have to look up to something that is greater than you in order to become what you are meant to be."

"When you are open and willing to change, you will move out of your own way."

"You can't always listen to what your heart or mind says, but you can always listen to your soul. It is older and wiser than the heart and mind."

"Some spirits are not meant for you to understand, but only to experience."

"The way out of a situation is never what you thought it would be, but the situation can be solved given the right frame of mind."

"The manifestation of something great can be achieved if you allow yourself to be receptive to the positive entities."

"Being you is the only requirement in, to, and for life."

"Always let the colors of your personality make a difference to someone whose life is in black and white."

"If you're going to make a 'noise' in life, make sure it is a positive one."

"If you don't understand something well enough, do not be intimidated, but allow yourself to be aware of the things you need to know."

"The challenges that you face today are making room for the person you will become."

"Life can be a garden, but you must choose to plant the first positive seed. Make that choice and start with you."

"Smile, because someone may need it to make it through their situation."

"The biggest mark you can leave on the world is being the greater individual that has been created in you."

"A state of confusion appears when you allow your outer man to direct the path for the inner man."

"No one is ever truly lost. They are just sorting through the 'mess' to discover a 'blessing' that has been with them all along."

"In the midst of your struggle, your purpose in life will be discovered."

"Intelligence is based off not what someone tells you but what you're able to gain from it; if you apply it to your life, then wisdom becomes the byproduct of the experience."

"People who play 'games' have difficulty living in real life."

"Some people are happy and content with their excuses. They are too afraid and too prideful to realize that if you remove the excuses better results in your life will emerge."

"If you are too busy contemplating the truth, then you are delaying the process of discovering who you are and what you can accomplish."

"You have the unique ability to smell change. Don't cover your face in order to block it out. It will always find a way in."

"Your greatest allies are those who can truly see your potential even when you decide to put on sunglasses to block it out."

"If someone cannot understand the wavelength that you are on, it just means the station you are on is not meant for them to tune into."

"Life is like making a cake. You provide the necessary ingredients, but it is what you use to hold everything together that matters."

"There is something more, but you have to be willing to become what has already been placed in you."

"Always be on a mission to be better."

"Always be involved in the re-creation and the realization of you. Nobody knows your story like you do."

"It only takes a millisecond to realize the issues you have can be fixed. It can go from mistakes made to lessons learned to wisdom being established."

"Be so busy redefining yourself that others will look at you and want the same for themselves."

"If you don't want to be a puppet of this world, then find the strength and have the faith to burn those strings and become who you are meant to be."

"People are going to want you for something, but there is 'ONE' who truly deserves you. Discernment provides clarity."

"Every time you speak some positivity in another person's ear, a blessing is soon to follow."

"When you start craving 'truth,' it just means you have surpassed a level of bullshyt that most do not graduate from."

"You should be so focused on creating a better you that bullshyt and drama have no choice but to take a rain check."

"Some things have to become secondary in order for you to be primary."

"The most important things in your life are screaming for attention. In order to handle them properly you must click the mute off and turn up your volume for a better understanding."

"The more you are tested and the more experience you gain, the more you get the opportunity for wisdom to come to fruition."

"Never be what people expect you to be, but only what they wish they could be."

"Sometimes you have to empty yourself of everything you know, everything you've learned, and everything you've grown accustomed to in order to make room for the things you need to make you into a better, stronger, lovable, and wiser person."

"As women, we are the earth, and in order for things to grow we have to be receptive."

"Some people are not meant to evolve at the same rate as you."

"If you understand the value of kindness, you should give it to those who need it the most."

"Your soul has a longer memory than your mind. Trust your soul."

"If you try to pretend with your feelings you will be senseless."

"Your soul was not created to do temporary things, so you have to feed it with temporary peace, happiness, and love."

"Some people are so quick to tell your story because their story is missing some chapters."

"Seek out the same likeness that your soul is attracted to."
"Once you understand your uniqueness, no one can box you in."

"Some things are meant to be understood from a distance for a reason. Not everyone can handle things at face value."

"Otherworldliness is something people yearn to find."

"Some don't know how to shine in the light because they are used to the shade surrounding them."

"You cannot look at people with half of your vision and expect to get the full picture of who they are."

"When you start to become unattached to certain things in this life, your shoulders will be weightless."

"Just because it is cold doesn't mean you have to be bitter on the inside. Forgiveness is best felt when you learn how to warm up your own heart; then it will flow to the better parts of you."

"Have enough life experience to add to your wisdom."

"There are so many beautiful things to see that are not wrapped up in human form or in a location. Discover what they are and enhance your life."

"You can't be ready to handle business if you refuse to dress up your intelligence."

"Sometimes the physical eye needs to be blinded in order for the spiritual eye to be more defined."

"The spirit of change will come to you when you are ready to accept what is and do away with what was."

"When you are awakened to your purpose...start to move forward in faith."

"Life becomes flexible when you adapt and learn to bend with it."

"Having an infectious spirit changes people, places, and things."

"Trying to shrink your mental capabilities to the mundane is equivalent to trying to sharpen a pen in a pencil sharpener."

"Sometimes stepping out of your realm will lead to other places your soul has dreamed of."

"If you can activate the truth, imagine what it would be like when you make it tangible and deliver it to the seeker."

"Once you discover your best ability, increase it, share it, and wear it with pride."

"To know what you want in a world that doesn't is a true blessing."

"Discover those things that are sincerely worth it."

"Tell the truth not to boost your ego and stroke your pride but to bring peace to your mind and clarity to your soul."

"Learn to separate yourself from those things that bring you no good and no love."

"The struggle has no color."

"Some people are only meant to be spectators in your life, while others are meant to be active participants."

"If you give peace you will get peace back."

"Everyone doesn't elevate at the same speed."

"How are you going to fight for number one when you're fighting for number two?"

"People do small favors for you every day, some good and some bad. Thank them for the lesson you never knew you needed to learn."

"Some people will not be able to handle you at full throttle will slam on the brakes and hit reverse."

"Never be scared of growth because you never know what beautiful thing you're destined to be."

"A single thought could either start an action or cause a reaction."

"Nobody is ever too big or too small to learn something."

"You cannot be afraid to level up…it's a process you have no control over."

"Every day we should strive to become more than the needle IN the haystack and find out why we don't need the haystack in the first place. You have an opportunity in the 'hole' of the needle than the barrier in a single piece of hay."

"If you do everything with a purpose you will add more meaning to your life."

"Life requires so little of you pay attention."

"When you show the bareness of your intelligence a piece of your soul gets into the mix."

"Always be kind to your enemies…it's another way to disarm them completely."

"If you have experienced the smell of the greatest pain it will open your nose to make you wake up and realize that you need to start breathing in the truth."

"The vision that you have for yourself needs to be bigger than the environment that you are currently living in."

"If you ever find yourself stuck on 'mute' emotionally, physically, spiritually, and mentally, it's time to just change the batteries. Changing the batteries can make things you are pressing toward simple."

"Never bring a storm into someone's life, because they may be battling a storm that is much stronger than you think. Be mindful, be considerate, and learn how to be the peace in the midst of that storm."

"People say they want change, but do they have the courage to embrace and accept the change that is required to move beyond the human limitations and expectations? The change adds to the foundation to make it stronger and wiser, whereas negative change puts a crack in the foundation."

"People do not realize that the type of weather they put on the path to that city on the hill dictates their acceleration to that blessing."

"The meaning of forever doesn't reside in a person, place, or thing but rather in what you love. Something like that cannot be defined in a book."

"In order to do better, feel better, look better, and understand things better you must first move out of your own way. Go beyond what you see. Ego cannot go where you are trying to journey to."

"Before you can speak something into existence externally, you must breathe it into existence internally. You must breathe first in order to speak."

"If you live a life positively it will act as a repellent against negative things that try to attack you."

"The beauty in an enigma is that the mystery offers new things to be discovered, taught, and shared."

"There is a higher calling, a higher meaning, and a higher level to understanding, but in order to receive it you must answer the call, digest the meaning into your system, and comprehend the message in your mind."

"When you find your reason/purpose, sometimes the only thing you can do is smile!"

"The difference between doing the right thing and the easy thing is one will have more of a fulfilling outcome that will sit well with your soul, and a lesson will be learned as well."

"Your greatest strength always comes from the most unlikely source."

"With all your battles, be determined to come out victorious."

"We will never know why a person may fall, but we must have enough love and compassion to understand when and how that person rises. When we fully comprehend it, the why becomes irrelevant."

"Be strong enough not only to stand side by side with someone but also to go toe to toe with them. Be smart enough to know when they can lean on you and you can lean on them. You need a partner who truly complements you on every level, not a partner who makes things complicated."

"If you educate yourself it will enable you to consciously elevate others. We are not meant to be one-dimensional when we live in a multi-dimensional world."

"When you surround yourself with basic individuals, you can expect basic results."

"Some things are not meant to be thought out in a logical sense. It's those rare occasions when you have to go with what feels right on a soul level."

"You cannot embrace something in its entirety with the door being cracked open only a little bit."

"Growth is not optional but mandatory to your being."

"Greatness will require you to make certain moves that some will never comprehend. There is a different type of greatness in everyone; it just takes the right spirit to let it loose."

"Sometimes you have to cut and uproot yourself from soil that is no longer fertile and positive for your lifestyle. Great pain will push you to seek out soil that can heal and help you grow, but you have to want it."

"You cannot make someone see who is willing to be blinded by all the things that need to be learned but refuses to make the move that will benefit their life."

"Some do not realize when their time is up and the role that they once played in another's life is done. Every action has a reaction and bad motives will never produce good intentions. No love is ever lost, but you do love that person with a different perspective."

"Surround yourself with those who know what pain is and learn, grow, and heal from it, rather than those who pretend that pain does not exist, learn nothing, and hinder the healing process."

"When you meet those who vibrate at the same frequency, as you both come together you will vibrate higher. However, those with a low frequency do not realize how low it truly is. You have to want, crave, and desire a higher frequency. No one can do that but you; you cannot fake energy, nor frequency."

"You can lose something great by having mediocre thoughts, actions, and words. You are meant to elevate and then resonate with another soul."

"Mistakes are just lessons to be learned to help you get to the next level in life. There are no extra lives, there isn't a pause button, there is no turning off the game, and, most importantly, there is no human on earth who can take your controller and play your life for you. So pass the lesson yourself and elevate. You were created to stay on one board and that is why there are levels to this thing called life."

"Nothing in life is ever on a part-time basis. Life is and will always be full-time. Learn what you can so you can grow into the full-time individual you are meant to be. Living on a part-time basis is not productive to your soul."

"You cannot go in deep with someone who isn't ready to start digging. Digging requires you to get through the mess so you can retrieve the blessing."

"If you knew how sweet the end of the journey would be then you would embrace the sourness of the process. Everything done in life has a sweet and sour taste to it. If you understand that then you can digest anything."

"When people can't figure out the reason behind your smile they automatically assume a person, place, or thing did it. When it was really you who decided to have unlimited happiness in your life. Smile because you can."

"At this point in time, surround yourself with those who can speak to your inner you. Your outer part is just for decoration."

"Sometimes the biggest mountain you have to climb over is yourself, the deepest river you have to cross is the tears that fall at a rapid pace from your face, and the biggest chain to break from is the one that keeps your mind hostage."

"Be bold in every positive thing that you do in your life, and once you do that, tell your non-believers, critics, and even your ego to have a seat. Greatness, happiness, and courage require something much deeper, and it's called faith."

"The journey is never easy, simple, or fast, but you meet the hard parts so you can finally embrace the aspects of life that are simple. The difficult parts increase with each step taken so you can have an appreciation and love for the simple things, and taking things slowly is to show you that nothing can be done fast. The lesson is to accept and internalize every part of the journey."

"Never get to the point where you are so unhappy that you want to clip another person's wings. We all have the right and the freedom to fly but we need the strength of our wings to do so."

"Not everyone is qualified to be an active participant in your journey. Some are only meant to be spectators and observe in order to learn something valuable; only active participants will vibrate at the same frequency as you."

"When your only concern is with your own elevation you become uninterested in the things that are still sitting on the ground; it is called growth."

"Bless someone with your smile, let your laugh be an inspiration, and show your courage to help another on their way."

"The strength of your soul can determine what attributes your character will show."

# Love

"If I can love a little better and little harder…I will."

"A heart that loves more freely is a heart more often."

"Those who love the hardest, accept all the flaws, and compromise experience the worst pain."

"The greatest tragedy is to love unconditionally and never receive love in return."

"It is simple to love yourself, but the greatest difficulty is loving someone else."

"I know for myself that the best part of me is the way I love."

"From believing to knowing, love is the center of my being."

"If there is one thing that I have done right in my life it is the way I love unconditionally."

"Having the ability to love shows what type of person you are."

"Never deny yourself love; it's like cutting off your air supply."

"Some people lack the ability to do anything extraordinary with their lives, and then there are others who do extraordinary things by loving those who can't see a way of loving themselves."

"Never lie to your own heart, for when the truth appears it won't recognize the feeling."

"Love will elude you every time if you don't pay close attention to it."

"It's sad when you love someone and they know it, sense it, and can feel it, yet push everything to the back burner. Love is not meant to be one-sided and you don't know how much damage you are doing to that one person. Love responsibly, not recklessly."

"In order to love there is something much more that is required other than a verbal confirmation."

"Just because your moods change doesn't mean your ability to love should."

"Love is the ultimate illusionist. Sometimes you see it and sometimes you don't."

"The greatest obstacle to overcome is allowing yourself to love another unconditionally."

"Find love in everything that you do and you will discover that love never left you. You just had a difference of opinion and had to find your way back to it."

"You know you love yourself when you start to get on your own damn nerves."

"Some people will never understand the reason behind the way you talk and walk. Some will guess and fail, and then there is always the one person who truly gets it because they have been paying attention all along…that's an unspoken love from the beginning."

"If you are afraid to love then you are afraid to live. You have to love to live and live to love. Love is essential and the key to opening everything."

"Having the best does not include the material things life has to offer. Simply being God-driven, of good heart, and spiritually grounded, and having peace of mind, is what makes you abundantly rich beyond anything you can imagine. Some people lack the ability to see those rich things in their heart, and I am glad I'm able to see them in the people I know and love."

"In a world where people are so focused on outer beauty, there will always be someone who is in tune with your wavelength and can see your inner beauty without having to see your face."

"Only real love can heal true love."

"If you don't feed your soul and give it what it needs, a little bit dies every day. If you don't give or put love in your heart, your heart will forget what love feels like."

"When someone tells you they miss you…believe them; when someone shows you they really care…accept them; when someone shows you general concern without looking to gain anything but your company and smile….cherish them. Kindness is a gift that should be treated like a blessing."

"You do not need a reason to love or care about someone. Love and care about them regardless of whether they know about it or not."

"One of the best things about knowing what your flaws are is that it shows that you accept the fact that you are not perfect, you have identified how to make the changes, and you love yourself enough that you want to be a better person."

"What makes you beautiful is that you accept yourself for who you are, not for what you want to be like or whom you want to be like or impress. Being beautiful is something from within. Begin to accept your beauty by accepting yourself as the individual that you are."

"If you pretend to love someone, you are only preventing yourself from experiencing the pure essence of it."

"Love is a verb and so much more than a noun."

"Define yourself on your own terms and no one else's. Love yourself in your own unique way so that people want to love the way you do."

"The most important and key element of love is you."

"Love never gives up on us; it's we who give up on love."

"Finding what your passion is in life…that's true love."

"Love requires a level of vulnerability that few people are cut out for."

"Another idea of love is the ultimate sacrifice."

"True and pure love is the music of our lives."

"To see love in the person you care for and appreciate means more than a thousand words ever spoken before."

"Love has a way of caressing and soothing the soul that allows another to experience it in its purest form."

"Regardless of what anyone tells you, happily ever after does exist when you believe in true love."

"Love is like when snow falls…no matter when and how it happens, you will know because you will be covered in it."

"Love is and can be the most positive force in your life if you allow it to be."

"Love should be as easy as breathing. If you can't breathe then the love isn't there."

"Love is a living entity that needs to be fed and nourished in the same manner as you would any other living thing.

"To grow and not know what true love is…is a tragedy in itself."

"If love was easy to acquire then it would be easy to hold."

"Your appetite for love should be as strong as your appetite to live life."

"To love unconditionally is living life in its best form."

"The love of people is like an acquired taste: you will either like it the first time or you won't try it again."

"To accept life in all forms is to allow love in all forms."

"To drive one insane is to love them regardless of their faults."

"In the arena of love, everyone wins!"

"Some things are better meant to be understood; love is meant to be felt."

"Things that you can fathom with your mind should be felt in your heart and connect with your soul."

"Some people fail to realize the importance of a smile, the sweetness felt in a hug, and the gratitude in a simple gesture. Always show love in any given form!"

"Never allow anyone to destroy your ability to demonstrate your type of love. Your love is unique and special in its own way."

"Love allows you to live more freely."

"Having a big and loving heart has its own rewards and consequences."

"Sometimes it takes a number of heartaches to realize what your true Achilles heel is."

"I lack the ability to hate because my capacity to love and give peace is so great within me."

"Find your reason to love, to hope, and to live again."

"Find the passion you seek and love more abundantly with love as your guide."

"In order to live a more genuine life you must do things from the heart. The first step is to be good to yourself and then to others. Your heart will tell you the next steps; just have faith."

"Hardening your heart shuts out love from entering."

"Never lose yourself to someone who has no intent on getting lost with you. If they choose to get lost with you then that's love."

"The only song a heart knows is when love is present in the melody."

""Love has the ability to build or self-destruct, so use it wisely."

"In order to understand what love is, you must embrace the essence that it gives off."

"Some live their whole lives not knowing or experiencing the full potential of love."

"As long as you have love in your heart, there is no room for hate to fill."

"If you put a crack in someone's trust, make it your business to repair the damage with love in sincerity."

"Love has no secrets and no enemies."

"There is no defense against love because it always wins."

"The most beautiful things are better felt when love is present."

"If you are tuned into love, you won't go searching for another channel."

"Love will test you to make sure you are worthy of it."

"The purest thing that is created in absolute perfection is love."

"Love brings a certain level of peace and awareness unique to every individual that allows it to take up residence in the heart, mind, and soul."

"To understand love better you must first surrender and be vulnerable."

"It is best to let aspects of love be."

"Pure love is not confined by the ideals of man."

"It is better to concentrate on how love is than what love is."

"To love is to allow your heart to beat outside of you and be held by someone you love deeply."

"To accept all the flaws and faults of another is to love them in your current state of mind and feeling."

"No matter how deep the hurt has been, love is able to heal it and make it whole once more."

"When God is omnipresent so is love."

"Love is always a guaranteed thing when it is coming from a loving person."

"There is no time limit on when love starts or when it finishes."

"If love was more like the wind, we would feel it on our face more often."

"To experience the full measure of love, you have to leave yourself open to receive it."

"Love is never in competition with anything."

"Sometimes you have to discover new methods of love and then see how people truly are."

"One of the most unfortunate things that can occur is when love is given and not reciprocated."

"Sometimes you have to get over yourself in order to love yourself better."

"It's best to admit when you are in love rather than deny it. Your heart is only doing what is natural."

"What makes a person more beautiful is when you see love all over their face."

"Being able to see how a person loves speaks volumes about how they are."

"There is never a bad time to tell someone how much you love them."

"When the heart desires love, give it what it wants and don't be a fool."

"It's OK to forget what you've been through, but always remember the love that was given."

"You have to understand that love is not going to come when you want it but when you need it the most."

"Love clears everything you thought you knew about it and replaces it with a feeling worth having."

"When you knowingly embrace your faults, you are in the process of making yourself stronger, wiser, and open to love."

"To love openly is to reward your heart and soul."

"Love is only hindered by our own human condition."

"As the warm sun shines on you, that is the effect that love has."

"Love: living with your faults and meeting someone who has their own faults, and working together to cancel them out and experience a new form of communal self-love."

"Within the boundaries of love, you will find another level of patience and understanding."

"Always seek love in its real form."

"Some things are meant for you to hold on to, while other things need to be let go of in order to grasp something much better."

"Love should be held in a delicate fashion so it is not destroyed."

"The next level of love always requires a piece of you to be sacrificed."

"To be embraced by love is to know how special you are."

"Love is only a thought and feeling away from actuality."

"By suffocating love you keep it from growing and reaching those who seek it."

"The eyes of love look different on everyone."

"Love never gives up; it's very persistent."

"There is so much love in a smile one may never fully realize it."

"Being blessed is knowing when something is truly for you. Love is a blessing and should be treated as such."

"Love has a certain level of respect that some understand and embrace while others are too stupid to comprehend its an awareness and higher grade of appreciation."

"Have enough sense to love and enough sense to banish hate."

"Love is not about weakness but about strengthening."

"Having a deeper understanding of yourself will give you access to loving yourself more."

"The best definition of love is when 'you' are a part of it."

"Love is such a powerful entity, so be careful how you use it. It should never be flung around like a wet T-shirt that desperately needs to wrung out."

"You can only give what your heart will allow."

"There should be no room to judge, only to love."

"Always put your energy toward those who challenge you into being better, bring positivity to your life, and love you unconditionally."

"In order to love someone you have to do the impossible."

"There is nothing equivalent to love but love."

"A person should be good for all angles of you and not just pleasing to certain things. Either love a person all the way or none of the way."

"Your heart is capable of so many things; to put limitations on it cages it."

"Actions of love speaker louder than words of love."

"There is a certain level of peace that is given from a person who has a loving spirit, a kind word, and a pure heart."

"Love calls us to be many wonderful things, and stupidity is not one of them."

"In order for love to be abundant in your life, truth must be at its foundation."

"Loving someone while they are dealing with their 'mess' speaks volumes about the type of heart and love you have and give. The greatest reward is when the person who has their 'mess' can have the strength to love you."

"To love those who genuinely care about you while you're in your process of healing means the love you have is in the process of transforming your heart to make it stronger."

"To deny yourself the purest form of love is equivalent to knowing your potential and never realizing your dream."

"Pure love and understanding comes through when you least expect it to help enhance you and your life."

"To fall in love is easy but to grow in love is one exceptionally jarring journey that only few have travelled."

"Love is not supposed to hurt but rather to enhance your life."

"The type of love you are able to give is specific to you. It is written in a style and language that some may never understand, but there is always the 'I' who will find the true beauty and essence in it and will give it back to you doubled."

"To love someone's soul is the beginning of unconditional love."

"To know peace is to discover love, and in discovering love you find peace."

"Love can be your greatest teacher if you take the time to listen to its genuine message."

"No matter how hard you try to fight it, deny it, and hide it, love always has a way of coming in and changing everything you thought you knew. Embrace the change and live life positively."

"The best kind of love is the kind that is not asked for but is given without questioning and is genuine."

"To have no hate toward another is unconditional love."

"All the love songs sung can never describe the love I have for you."

"To be a lover of the soul is to look beyond the tainted flesh."

"If you want to love the world you must first love yourself."

"Your heart recognizes the truth even when you are not ready to accept it."

"You never know the unconditional love you are capable of until you feel it."

"Unconditional love is not a foreign concept because we experience it every day without knowing it."

"A soul in love is forever concrete in the eyes of God."

"Love is a free form devoid of space that is shaped by how you want it to be. It's own level of energy and giving it to anyone or anything that is brave enough to decide to embrace it. Love is what you desire it to be so let your love be a positive force and let it make you evolve into something greater."

"Always let love define love. No human definition or permission is ever required."

"The only way to repay love is with love…no substitution."

"You have to learn how to love your own heart in its entirety before attempting to love someone's heart."

"Love in its truest form has no regrets, nor does it make mistakes."

"Be someone's forever instead of their backup."

"True love is when you fall for someone's intellect and soul first."

"Love doesn't know to be anything else but full-time."

"If you never truly mastered the art of love, then how would you know the real thing if it showed its face?"

"You cannot run or hide from the eternal love that you are meant to have."

"Love is easy with the right spirit involved."

"The moment you realize what your heart has known all along, you become the embodiment of love."

"Love requires that you take the first step."

"If you are afraid to experience love then you fail to appreciate what it can bring to your life."

"Those who love with their soul know how to love on another plane of existence."

"A soft heart cannot understand a chaotic spirit but can heal it with love."

"Make sure you fall in love with the person and not their potentiality."

"The most beautiful thing in life is to give love, and the ugliest thing you can do in life is not give love back. Someone may need the way you love. Don't be in your own way and block your blessing."

"When a person truly and genuinely loves and cares about you they will learn to appreciate the storm and the rainbow within you. However, they will understand the reason behind both."

"Surround yourself with people who know how to use the 'L-word' properly. Who value the time in your presence, who force you to be better than what you are, and who have no other motive than to be a true friend and to see you happy."

"Some people fail to remember that the only thing that is unconditional is love. Everything else has a time stamp and at some point will expire."

"Those things that are meant to change you for the better will resonate with your soul, challenge your mind, and be of unconditional vibration of love."

"Love lasts longer when you fall for that person's intellect and soul first. Everything else will follow."

"What you are and have should be the only motive in order to be a true friend and to see others happy."

"Love is not difficult; it's when humans get ahold of it that makes it hard."

"To love hard is one thing that is an enigma in itself, but to love easy is a misconception, because if it was or is 'easy' then it would be something everyone would do naturally."

"One of the greatest lessons that you could ever teach yourself and truly understand is that there is no right or wrong way to love."

**God**

"Every time you hinder someone's spiritual-growth process, you can cripple your own spiritual awareness."

"When God decides to do something, He does it in such a slight way that you do not realize it until the very end."

"Never underestimate your God-given abilities…He gave them to you for a reason."

"Sometimes you have to sit back and digest all the things God reveals to you in your current mental state."

"In order to go to that higher level of consciousness you must listen to that small, still voice."

"My soul and spirit are connected to my temple so I'll behave like a child of God."

"God gave us a certain kind of spirit and it's our responsibility to nurture it."

"Never question God's reasoning; His eyes are better focused on what's ahead."

"Even if I don't understand anything else in my life, God knows the purest angles of my heart."

"Sometimes God has to burn something in order to resurrect something and make it new."

"God works in the small and simple, so pay attention."

"When your heart, soul, and mind are in complete agreement with each other, it's a level of peace no human can fully understand."

"God will provide you with someone who will not only walk the spiritual path with you but will help expand your conscious mind."

"God is the ultimate stand-up comedian."

"God knows your thoughts before you can formulate an opinion."

"If God wants you to have it, He will provide the increase where He sees fit."

"Pay attention to what is in front of you, because God is about to bless you before you blink."

"A God-conscience is required on the road to the spiritual path."

"If you deny love into your heart, you are denying God's spirit to fill your soul. How thirsty are you?"

"Sometimes God will provide you with exactly what you need in any given form. It is up to you how you perceive it and if you accept it."

"You cannot set yourself up for failure when God has already planned the victory."

"God does something new in your life every day and it's up to you to discover what it is. It's never the obvious, and requires looking deeper."

"No one has the authority to question the path God has chosen for you. Your path is for you and no one else. To attempt to even explain it is pointless because the path is written in a language only you understand."

"God will test you at different levels in your life. It's up to you to pass the lesson in order to understand the message you need to learn."

"In the midst of your silence, trials, and tribulations, God is blessing you so you can live more abundantly."

"That instant that you find yourself quiet and the moment is beautiful is where you can see and hear God making moves in your life. It's not 'a coincidence' or 'by chance'; it's all by God's calculation."

"God will give you exactly what you need when you are least expecting it. The good that God does for you means He took a peek into the desires of your heart and granted the increase."

"Things will happen to you that will read 'give up' on so many different levels, whether it is verbally or subconsciously. At that pivotal moment you must tap into that God-consciousness and encourage yourself. God did not give you the ability to 'give up' but rather the ability to keep going.'"

"Daily interactions with God will bring forth an abundance of blessings."

"God's dwelling place is in you and around you."

"Sometimes as a person you need to know the best parts of you. Not because someone pointed them out but because you discovered them for yourself. I know without a doubt that my best part is not what I can do but what I give from the heart, which is love. God knows your heart because He made it."

"Sometimes there is not going to be an explanation for everything that happens in life, but if you have common sense and understand that your faith will lead you to the Source, then you are halfway to the answer."

"There are certain things in life you should know, and if you don't, then ask God to provide the increase in those special areas. Always seek God regardless of your circumstances."

"When you wake up feeling determined, God has turned on something inside you that says 'keep going.'"

"God has a particular way of showing you what is for you and what is not. If you are tuned in, you will be able to tell what frequency He is on and receive the message. If not, then you are clearly on the wrong channel. Know the difference between the two and make the necessary changes."

"Things will only come to you when you are ready to receive them. It's not about your timing but is God's timing. Remember, God is not going to bless you with something if He knows you are ready."

"Learn something new about yourself every day, and if you come across something you don't like, then you have the power to make the change. You are dynamic and never become static. If you're static, you will not grow."

"God will give you the desires of your heart; just make sure what is in your heart is sincere and true. God knows your heart because He made it."

"When God has His hands in your life nothing is by coincidence, by chance, or by luck. He allows things to fall as they should because His vision is not blurred but is perfectly fixed on the plans He has for you. No plan is better than God's plan."

"When you deny your heart something it desires, it is the equivalent of walking in darkness and seeing the light but never allowing your spirit to reach it."

"When you recognize and accept that you are a work in progress, certain things will fall into place beautifully and effortlessly. Stay open and stay connected to the Source, because He is working it out for your good."

"God is not always going to give you something that you are going to love. He will give things that will try you, upset you, test you, bless you, and sustain you. He doesn't do these things for no reason at all, but rather wants to see you triumph in the small things because He knows what is coming down the line. Every challenge is designed to increase your faith, so pay attention."

"The most beautiful and genuine-hearted people do not come into your life by accident or coincidence. Know the difference when God puts them in your life for a reason, and be good to them, because God didn't have to do it!"

"God allows certain things to fall into place perfectly and some things to fall apart by His decision. It's up to us to recognize what was let go and to know what will be."

"Sometimes the best person for you comes out of nowhere but has been there all along, certain things just fall into place with no effort, and the simple things bring out the most joy. When God reveals a genuine person in your life be sure to pay attention to all the details, because that's where your blessing is."

"Whether or not you have found your passion in life, just remember that it is going to change you mentally, physically, emotionally, and spiritually. Embrace it with everything in you; after all, God wants you to have the best!"

"God has given you the capacity and the ability to do and be whatever you want with His guidance. You would be a fool not to take full advantage of it, and once you find your ultimate passion. handle your business. Love, cradle, and embrace who you are capable of being, regardless of what others say. No one knows the power of your mind."

"Most things start off small because hope is involved, but it is faith that is leading it."

"God provides us with everything that we need, but it's our human side that thinks we need more than what we have."

"God did not create you to be closed in any shape or form. He created you to be open and receptive so you might learn and others might learn from you."

"Never pretend or act like you know everything, but what you do know is this: God made your mind, heart, and soul. He gave you the mind to do what you know is right, the heart to love others unconditionally, and the soul to be close to him."

"Some people are destined for greatness and some are destined for something more than greatness. The difference between the two is that you're driving a vehicle whose tank either has nothing in it or is filled with God's promise. Which one fits you?"

"The greater the conflict is, the greater the transformation will be. There is a blessing in between the conflict and the transformation, and that's where being silent is required."

"What gives me the most hope every day is God's grace: knowing that His grace is going to give me the strength for whatever I face, and knowing that nothing is a surprise to God."

"When you start treating people as a hobby it says a lot about you. If you have no respect for humanity, including yourself, and you play with emotions like a pair of dice, you need to engage in some serious introspection, and you need to seek God, because it's obvious you are severely broken."

"You have your good and bad days, you still smile in spite of it, you give more than you receive, you care when you shouldn't, you give people the benefit of the doubt when you know they don't deserve it but you won't complain. You know God is working it out for your good and He knows the desires of your heart...and that's enough for you!"

"Sometimes God has to strip you of everything in order to build you back up."

"Some things in life can be taught while other things are given solely by the Creator. You cannot force the Creator to give you anything that you have not put all your faith and trust in."

"Always allow peace to enter your domain and take up residence in your spiritual house."

"You as a failure is never in God's plan. He created you to be successful."

"Spiritual awareness is when you have your hand in God's hand and He is leading you up a path to what you are destined to be."

"Be a product of many positive things but be the ultimate product of a loving God."

"God has a jar of promises for you, so handle it with care because it's so fragile."

"There will always be obstacles in your way, but remember, God is a ladder over troubled things."

"When someone touches your soul it's because God allowed that person access to your secret treasure within without you knowing."

"When God blesses you, don't try and fight it, because God is going to have His way."

"When you place God in the number-one spot in your life, everything else will fall into place."

"God will find you in the midst of your chaos even though you placed yourself there."

"Never hurt the hand that is willing to help you, for that hand may never reach out again to help in your time of need. God's blessing was upon you and you pushed it away."

"Being committed to God will bring you more satisfaction than anything else."

"God will bless you to see things clearly and then the He will bless you to feel things more abundantly."

"God's addition and subtraction is better than men's division; apply the correct calculation to your life."

"Trying to figure out God's plans is like looking for keys in the dark."

"God already has everything figured out, so why not follow His lead?"

"When God wants your attention it happens in a subtle and small way."

"Never doubt God, because He doesn't have doubts when it comes to you."

"God's definition for you is yet to be revealed."

"Nothing is perfect but the spirit of God."

"God will provide you with permanent fixtures in your life. You have no business making changes to those permanent fixtures with temporary placeholders."

"When God makes renovations in your life He is preparing you for greater things."

"When God shows you who and what is for you, things will occur in the most natural way that your logic will not be able to decode."

"In God's class the one crucial requirement is to show and tell. He shows you how powerful He is in your life and He wants you to tell so others will know."

"When God gives you a glimpse of your future, take hold and walk boldly to your destiny in life."

"If you never acknowledge the blessing in the person God has provided for you He will overturn it and give your blessing to someone more deserving."

"God will force you to face your fears and realize the potential He has given you."

"Do what you love, love who you love, and be passionate about it. Do it with everything in you or nothing at all. Either give 100% or zero. That is how life is, and don't believe you can do something halfway, because God doesn't work like that."

"Never be less than what God has called you to be."

"Some people have difficulty recognizing their blessing when it comes."

"The best first relationship to have is one with God, and the second is with yourself."

"If you don't humble yourself, God will."

"If you have all your fingers and toes, then you can count some of the blessings you receive."

"God has yet to reveal the true definition of what you are."

"If there is something that you are lacking, God will let you know what it is."

"Running away from a good thing is running from a blessing that God wants you to have…stop running!"

"Do not presume to know anything unless God has provided you with the answer."

"God has your best interests at heart because He is the one who created them and it."

"Love those who will love you right and ignore those who hate you with all their might. And know God has got you as long as you stay in His sight."

"God gives you little victories every single day. Try your best to recognize them and the happiness they provide."

"When God decides to humble you, it is going to be in a way that you never expected or thought of. He does it in such a way that it will be a lasting memory and forever be a lesson you can apply every day to your life. So rest others good and be good to yourself, because He is writing all the time."

"Be so comfortable in your skin and love it right now, because people will ask where you bought it. Tell them, 'from my maker, God, and He has one in your size especially for you!'"

"You cannot grow emotionally, spiritually, physically, and socially by continuously having weeds come around you that latch on to draw on your life force. You may do a temporary fix to try to get rid of the weed, but you must uproot that negative anomaly immediately. You cannot grow using old ways, period. Everything must change in order for a better you to come to fruition. Surround yourself with positive-minded people who show and tell in their daily life. When you deal with a very positive individual, everything occurs naturally due to the peace that individual brings. There is no misconception, no other motive, no secrets…just the plain ole truth every single day. That individual only wants you to have the same level of peace, happiness, and complete understanding of how life is truly meant to be. Another definition for it is unconditional love in a higher form. You can't keep running and expect to grow naturally. Stop running and embrace the growth. The special individuals are not meant to grow at your speed, no matter how much you or anybody tries to influence them. You will be blessed for doing your part. You will grow according to God's speed. If you ignore, mistreat, or hurt the person God has put in your path, you already know what the consequences are. Grow into the individual God has intended you to be. Embrace those who love you inside and out regardless of how screwed up you might be…one is perfect, so love them back with everything you have inside you!"

"People will always forget the good that you do for them, but God doesn't so keep doing good and being blessed."

"Sometimes the journey that we must take has to be taken alone. Even though we want to have company with us, we can't. We are the writers of our dreams and God is the publisher. He has the rights to your journey and your dream."

"Never pretend to be other than what God has called you to be. Your changes are minor compared to the major changes God has for you."

"God gave you one heart but endless possibilities of showing love."

"God will let you have a taste of the desire of your heart. If He deems you worthy to have it He will bless you to experience its full flavor."

"Every particle in you has a natural course of action that is set to God's divinity of time. When the timing is right everything that you are truly meant to be will come to fruition."

"Some people cannot process a positive mind and spirit because they allow negative interference to corrupt the motherboard that God built!"

"You can't fight God or what God has for you. Either way He is ultimately going to have His way."

"Never ever be what people expect you to be or thought of you to be, because you should only be concerned with how God wants, needs, and calls you to be. A God-consciousness is required on all levels of human understanding. It's one thing to 'get it,' but to comprehend and apply it is truly something different."

"God will reveal certain truths to you, and it is up to you to take heed of what those truths are."

"If God has a blessing for you and wants you to have it and gives it to you openly, why wouldn't you accept it? God wants to bless you!"

"God's peace is everlasting, but when you experience that type of peace, calmness, and balance in a singular individual, recognize it for what it truly is…a blessing. The peace that particular individual brings to your life is another form of God's love."

"What God has for you is placed in front of you and therefore not behind you. Some need to speed up or fall back and go at their own pace. The race is given to those who know they are blessed!"

"When God gives you something so precious and special, handle it with care. If you mishandle it, God will take it and deliver it to someone who is more qualified to handle it."

"The way God has you set up and how your future is planned, all you see is success, abundance of love, and happy times; therefore, there is no space for failure, heartache, or doubt."

"Man will plan so many things against you. Always remember that as long as you are thriving on the goodness of God, all the plans man concocts will be obsolete, destroyed, burned asunder, whisked away, and buried in the desert because God heard all your sincere prayers."

"How much of God do you have in your gas tank? If running on 'E,' you probably need to fill it up."

"Your spiritual growth depends on your attitude toward your inner man."

"Uncertainties in life allow God's opportunities to exist."

"Sometimes the frequency of life can be tuned into a station of nonsense, impractical anomalies, and negative juxtaposed situations that will force you to seek the station of God."

"The beginning of peace can come from an understanding heart, mind, and spirit."

"To crave another's soul is to seek out the divine that lies within."

"God is always looking for opportunities to bless you in your words and actions. If you are not careful you could miss out on a blessing that is meant to change your life for the better."

"Life has a set of rules and God has His own set of rules. Choose wisely!"

"Why get stuck in a remedial class of life when God has given you the tools to pass."

"Let loose those things that hold you back from reaching the potential God has set in you."

"If you know the waves in your life, eventually you will come upon a shore that God has created for you."

"The light that God has designed and created for you was not just for you to hold but to help those whose light has gone out."

"God's purpose for you is waiting for you to discover it."

"Sometimes things cannot be defined by outer beauty but by the spirit that is contained within. There lies the true sight of seeing something beautiful."

"Some people are not worth the tape that is keeping them together. The true nature of it is that the bonding agent needed is faith and the power of God to keep everything intact."

"Sometimes the only pattern you need to see is not what man has intended for you but what God has destined you to become. While man is predictable in common things, God is unpredictable in blessing you in what you need the most."

"Never be too busy to share a blessing God has given you."

"If you work hard for God, He will work harder and stronger for you."
"The only perfect love that exists is when God decides to bless you when you feel you don't deserve it."

"God's ability to change you will be more profound than man's ability."

"God is not complex but our mental state presumes that He is."

"God will sometimes put a mess in front of you to see who will clean it up. Will it be your inner man or your outer man? A choice that you have to make, because God is already there to make sure you clean it up properly."

"God will only allow you to do so much before He steps in to take over."

"Life will challenge our inner and outer man on all known and unknown levels."

"If God lays it out plainly for you to see, then you would be a fool not to follow it."

"Life has a funny way of reminding you whom you belong to."

"God has a certain level of unpredictability that always works in your favor whether you want to believe it or not."

"Life will bring some causalities of war, a sense of false realities, some financial instabilities, but only God's spirituality can take you where you need to be."

"We are here to help someone transition to another level of cognitive thinking and spiritual identification."

"Never doubt the power that God has given you. It increases daily without you truly knowing when, where, why, and how!"

"Sometimes God will create a snowball effect in your life to clear some room for what you need."

"Sometimes you have to sit in your own silence in order to hear your spirit talk to you."

"God will prepare you for exactly what you need and then bless you with what you deserve."

"If you put a good word of positivity in someone's ear from the heart, they will remember it and God will see it."

"God will turn you on to things that you will never need or want to shut off."

"God will send you people that resonate with more than just your heart but also with your soul."

"Your soul will always tell you exactly what you need and who you need."

"Some things are meant for you to see, touch, and smell, while others are better experienced on the soul level."

"Be good to those things that came back into your life. The Lord sent you a blessing."

"God will bless you when He knows you're ready."

"Believe that with every act of random kindness, every act done with your whole heart, God grants you a peace of spirituality that you would gain later but you would receive it now."

"Do what is required and God will provide the necessities."

"Never allow your soul to entertain a mediocre mess."

"Accept the responsibility of your own spiritual maturity."

"God shows us what true love really is. We don't fully understand until we are finally awake to accept it."

"You block your own blessing by being ignorant."

"Try being more of what God called you to be and much less of what ego and man says you need to be."

"God's sense of humor is longer than your lifespan."

"Sometimes your greatest heartache and disappointment will push you toward your greatest blessing. Your blessing is waiting for you at the crossroads of your journey. Have enough faith to continue on your path to meet your blessing."

"A man or woman that walks strong in faith and in conviction does not fear the wind or man but only God."

"God didn't create you and mold you to be basic."

"Some things are too good to be true. In that case, God is good, that is true, and so are His blessings that He gives. But why is it that when God sends a blessing we hesitate to be open and to extend our hand so our palm can receive the goodness? We need to get out of our own way and not be afraid. God wouldn't send a blessing if He thought you were not ready."

"Be careful how you treat a blessing that God has given you. God blesses us with certain people, places, and things for a particular reason. See the blessing for what it truly is, and if you mistreat it as quickly as God has given it to you He also has the power to remove it and give it to another."

"Some can go from hot to cold in so many ways. What would happen if God was just hot and cold with us? Be thankful we serve a God who runs on all temperatures and sees fit to bless us when we are hot and cold with others as well as ourselves."

"You will never have to be convinced or question whether God loves you or not. That beat in your heart is proof enough."

"Everything you could ever want in life know man cannot provide, but be thankful that we serve a God who can say yes, no, and wait. Yes to those things that your spirit needs, no to those things you think you need, and wait on the blessings that are about to happen."

"Sometimes your greatest strength does not come from listening, seeing, or thinking. It comes from the feeling of the whispers in the corridors of your heart. It is that vibrational spirit for you to be strong and encouraged."

"The race that you are running in is not to defeat your old self but to catch up to the ideal person God needs you to be. You will get tired, you will get frustrated, and you will find it difficult to breathe, but always remember that spirit will give you the wind you need to succeed."

"You will get more out of life when you give everything to God to handle it."

"That pivotal moment when you feel your strength has increased, your vision is clearer, your thoughts are more positive, your spirit is lighter, and your smile is brighter is when God removed an obstacle for that blessing to come through. Just wait on it, because it is coming!"

"As humans, at some point in our lives and on different occasions we are meant to fly. To fly not by the means of the physical or by that of transportation that can be used. To fly by letting go of the limitations that we create in our minds, releasing the hand that thought it was helping but was really holding you back from your true potential. In all realness, flying is taking an uncalculated risk that will reap benefits that will help you on your path. So today make up your mind to fly; fly by taking a leap of faith."

"Sometimes we go through different levels of spiritual deafness in our lives. Spiritual deafness happens when you have listened to the world too much about what it wants you to be. Spiritual deafness can be conquered when you turn away and listen for what God needs you to be. God shows and tells you exactly what you need, but you have to be fully tuned in. Take the headphones of the world off and listen for your destiny."

"The assurance of God is better than the advice of man."

"God does not make it difficult for us to seek Him out, but why is it that we make it difficult for ourselves to find Him?"

"Your words are more powerful than you think, especially when your spirit is right."

"There is no competition involved when God has already provided the increase that you need in your life. Pay attention to what is meant for you; it will be clear."

"There are two places God doesn't dwell in, and those are chaos and drama."

"God will place you in isolation sometimes, but it is only to prepare you for your destined elevation."

"Your happiness should never depend on man but only in God."

# ...And All The Other Bullshyt

"Even the simplest things have extraordinary abilities."

"The simplest things that are craved always seem to be the hardest to obtain."

"Always encourage others who found their passion, for they may inspire you to seek out your own."

"Good women are like buried treasure: after years of searching in the wrong places, X never marks the spot and they are always found in the most unlikely and unusual places."

"There is a certain beauty in being silent…no one ever knows what you're thinking and there is no expression on your face."

"Sometimes you have to face yourself in the mirror and say, 'I am not a quitter.'"

"Sometimes being too nice can be a hindrance because it allows room for bullshyt to come and take a seat."

"I care daily, constantly acknowledging real emotions."

"Every new leaf that grows is another opportunity to change, develop, and seek a new horizon."

"Looking someone in the eye is the first step in being honest."

"Appreciate what you do have because you could have nothing."

"Sometimes you have to know when to pump the breaks and when to go full steam ahead."

"Some people lack the ability to feel and think…I just lack the ability to fully give a shit."

"Always use your sense of logic to convey a clear message."

"Sometimes you have to find the beauty inside in order to find the beauty on the outside."

"It's better for you to have me as your teammate than as your competition, because you won't win."

"I think one of the most interesting things about being human is the ability to either care too much or not care at all. Some things you just can't do halfway."

"What parts of your life do you consider fiction or non-fiction?"

"It's hard to find the good when people have done you wrong."

"Everyone is entitled to a change in their season."

"I used to give people chances…not anymore. I am going to start charging."

"If you appreciate the value of a dollar, then you should appreciate it when someone gives you another chance to value it."

"Disappointment is like a shoelace coming undone: you see it happening and then you have to tie it back together and act like it didn't happen and walk on."

"You are gifted in so many ways, but dealing with bullshyt is not one of them."

"Know when you're being the equivalent of a dick."

"Never underestimate your ability to have asshole tendencies."

"Some people are not qualified to speak on your level."

"Some things are not meant for you to understand. Just be happy with the fact that you recognized, believed in, and experienced it for what it truly was."

"There are some things people miss and some things people just ignore and have difficulty knowing the difference."

"Being beautiful doesn't have anything to do with the physical, but rather with your mentality and spirituality."

"Sometimes it's better to keep the positive memories than to have a negative reminder around you."

"I'd rather be someone's single rose than be compared to a dozen roses."

"What makes me, and you, beautiful is not what is seen with the eyes but what is felt through the heart and the soul."

"Some people need to realize that when it comes to the number of chances given, there is a limit. If you hurt another person to the core, chances are you have reached your limit. A smart person wouldn't count the number of chances given, but a wise person would take the first chance and make it the last."

"Sometimes people will just not 'get you' no matter how hard they try, even if you try to explain it in layman's terms. It just means you are on a different level and people need to catch up to where you are."

"There are some people whom you should give up on and don't, and then there are others whom you shouldn't give up on who are really trying hard whom you give up on too easily. It is what it is!"

"Sometimes you need to 'slap' people with the truth because it will let them know to stop dreaming and that someone actually does care about them."

"True happiness does exist in the smallest things, but it is up to you to fine-tune your vision so you can see it."

"Fools and idiots are two different things; just make sure you know the difference."

"When you don't understand something, don't be ignorant about it but rather educate yourself to know instead of having doubt."

"Value what you have right now, because if you don't it will be someone else's treasure."

"When people miss the point of giving an apology, it shows that they didn't want to give it in the first place."

"Allow love to guide your path, nurture your spirit, and rest peacefully in your soul."

"Be careful of who and what you care about. It's not always guaranteed they will care back."

"When you start to expect too much from a person, it means that there is going to be an open doorway for disappointments."

"If you can't learn how to appreciate the little things, then how do you expect to appreciate the messenger?"

"Things are not always as complicated as they look…just change your perspective."

"If you know and embrace all your flaws, then people can't use them against you. Never give people the bullets to load their gun in order to take you out."

"Having the mind and determination to do the right thing can be difficult, but once you have done it the reward is all the sweeter and you will be at peace more often."

"When you have people who really know you and care truly for you, they will call you on your BS; thank them, because it gives you a chance to change it and be better!"

"In order to build on something you already have, make sure you use the experience and knowledge you gained to make it strong. If you don't, you are wasting your time; nothing lasts if you build with sand."

"If you have difficulty comprehending the small things, what makes you think you can digest the big things? Know what level you are on and try to elevate and not dissipate."

"I'd rather deal with people who are deep like oceans than those who continue to remain surface dwellers. One will provide growth and the other will have false pretenses."

"Some people are not qualified to be your friend, to sit in the passenger seat of your car, to rub elbows with you, or even to enjoy your company. It speaks volumes about your character but shows that you rise above the bullshyt, and also shows that the other person needs to grow up."

"Sometimes you have to leave people where they are so they can see where they need to go. You can learn so much about people from observation!"

"The wonderful thing about experience is that you have to put in the work in order to appreciate the true meaning of it. It's easier to say it than to do it."

"Never voice your opinion to an ear that did not ask for it by the lips. Even though all of our situations may have a similar story, it doesn't mean the characters are the same from beginning to the end. The experience of the challenge is unique to everyone."

"When you see someone happy, be happy for them. Don't criticize, pass judgment, make idiotic statements, try to 'figure it out,' or condemn them. Sometimes it takes some longer than others to reach a level of happiness. Happiness comes in many forms; make sure you know what form suits you best."

"While some may see you as regular, another will see you for the true beauty and genius that you are. While some may not understand your passion, another will be on your same wavelength. While some may not get the method to your madness, another has worked through the madness and created a method of their own."

"We are all diamonds in the rough, and once the diamond has been fully revealed it takes the right kind of person to care for it."

"Sometimes there are things in yourself that you are not supposed to see and are meant for others to recognize. Just because it's not clear to you doesn't mean it won't be clear to others."

"To understand anything you must go through something first. Experience is necessary in comprehending the small stuff."

"Being an artistic creature, I feel as though I lose a little bit of my mind in every piece of work I do, but I discover a part of myself that puts me in tune with my surroundings."

"Being intense (in a good way) on different levels is a good thing, but only to those who take the time to experience it. If someone is overwhelmed with one level, that means that they are not ready for the rest. But if someone can handle it you will know by them saying sincerely, 'I get it.'"

"There is something magical that happens when your soul is touched in an artistic way. Everything becomes so much clearer and even more beautiful."

"Compare every situation to a pair of jeans: if they are too tight…you can't walk right; if they are too loose…you have a little room to figure things out; if they fit just right…you have just enough balance to figure everything out. Don't worry if they are a little long—adjustments can be made—but if they are too short then you have to think about your next move."

"You should have enough sense to know who and what is good for you but be smart enough to recognize that every negative can be turned into a positive."

"The one thing that everyone has in common is karma. Either way you play your cards, karma is always going to be in your hand, so be careful!"

"You know someone is really full of shit when their words are > or < their own body language when it should be =...you do the math!"

"The best kind of message you can give to someone who does not listen is silence because they will discover they have to come up with their own conclusion as to why they did not listen the first time."

"People will never understand what you are saying and why you're saying it until they reach the level you are on, and then they will be able to fully comprehend the meaning of your words."

"People may mistreat you, say things about you, try to point out all your wrongdoings, break your heart, lie to you, etc. no matter what, and it's hard to never wish bad on another person. You may be mad as hell, but always be positive and wish them well because it will confuse them."

"Sometimes you have to walk in the rain like the sun is shining. Problems may pour down hard on you but you have to always remember the bright side of things."

"You should always have a craving to do more and the urge to be more than what you are right now."

"You should always wish friends and enemies well because your real friends know who you are, what you're about, and the path that you are on, but your enemies will not expect it and it shows that you are cut from a different cloth and you set yourself apart from everything else that is negative."

"Some people think that they deserve to be in the passenger seat of your life while you are driving. Certain things are required in order to be allowed to sit in that seat, and if they don't fit the requirements then they have no business being in your vehicle."

"How you talk and how you act should be consistent. Your mouth can say whatever you want but body language never lies. There must be a balance on all levels."

"The cards not being played are worth seeing and are held much closer!"

"What you don't say means more than what you say…choose your actions wisely!"

"Being far from ordinary does not make you weird but rather makes you truly unique in how you think, act, and talk. Strive to be different and not just blend in."

"Some people fail to realize that some things are meant to be simple and that they need to stop making other things complicated."

"When you lack the ability to view situations from all the given perspectives, you hinder yourself from learning and therefore growing. Never stunt your own growth process."

"Some things will ultimately fail because truth was not a part of the equation for a solution to present itself."

"Trying to follow the rules is one admirable quality, but breaking and creating new ones on your own terms is a passionate feat."

"Some will think they have you figured out until you flip the switch."

"Have the capacity to do what you say and say what you will do, because someone may be depending on you."

"You have to be a great friend to yourself before you can be a great friend to someone else."

"Be bold in all your endeavors because you leave a concrete footprint on those who remember you."

"When you feel positive, you will think positive."

"Never having a grip on reality leads to boundless episodes of disillusion."

"Never surround yourself with simple-minded people."

"We are our own hero and our own villain trapped in one body."

"Happiness is not defined by what others say or do but by your own strength of mind and actions."

"Even positive individuals have a limit on certain things. Never test that limit."

"If people cannot comprehend what you do and how you do it, it's because they never took the time to fully embrace you."

"In order for some things to make sense they need to fall apart so you can see what needs to be put back together and what doesn't fit."

"Just because you don't get the full picture doesn't mean there is no picture at all."

"Learn how to run free without the company of those who refuse to see and appreciate what lies ahead."

"Be humbled enough to know when love is honest and true and when sincerity is being offered, and have enough wisdom to understand when something is really for you."

"There are things meant for you and there are things that are meant to come from you."

"All artists are loners. It allows us to see the picture in a more colorful way, with which we can understand the world."

"When you are accustomed to having bad and you finally have something worthy you end up mishandling it."

"You know when someone is being a dummy and they don't realize it until it is too late."

"Sometimes you miss the person you met the first time and want them back."

"The narrower the path, the more chances you have to put one foot in front of the other to learn the lesson to get it right and never look back."

"Sometimes being someone's friend is a double-edged sword; either way you risk the possibility of getting cut."

"What can make a beautiful person ugly is a mouth full of lies."

"You don't understand the definition of strength until you have the experience of using it."

"As long as you do good by people on all levels, nothing bad can be said about you."

"Never say anything that you don't truly mean. The last thing you want to do is provide a genuine person with false hope and false pretenses."

"Always give people enough rope to hang themselves; when they finally realize what is happening, it is only because their lower half is going completely numb."

"When people are accustomed to dealing with the mediocre and the mundane they fail to realize, accept, and appreciate someone who is of value, worth, is consistent, understands loyalty, and breaths trust. If not they are doomed to go back to what they are familiar with."

"If you are not present during my struggle and low times don't even think you are going to be a part of my success in the future."

"When people expect a lie from you, surprise them with the truth."

"If your loyalty can be bought, then you do not understand its true value."

"Some people will try to blow smoke of nonsense at you, but it's up to you when you get tired and smother the fire that you are allowing to burn."

"Never bet against someone who has nothing to lose."

"Opening your eyes to the truth can be a blinding experience because of how bright the realness is."

"You have to want more for yourself than anything in the world."

"Some things are not meant for you to understand because your mind may not be equipped to handle that type of load."

"The goals that you set for yourself should inspire you to the point of electrifying your spirit to the driving force."

"Once you find that point of greatness in you, keep going and striving."

"Perfection is an illusion but dreams are real to a person who knows how to use them."

"Sometimes you have to protect yourself at all costs, and no matter what may present itself."

"The hardest thing a person can do is try to lie to their conscious mind when their subconscious knows the truth. You can't hush the truth from the inside."

"You have to stimulate the intellect first before making a physical connection."

"A simple solution to a perplexing question is to have enough sense to ask the Creator to provide the increase in your intellect."

"Perception is more than seeing things in a physical sense and needs cognitive realization and an emotional connection in order to bring life to a singular thought yet to be breathed into existence."

"A lie can never be spun into the truth no matter how many times you try to weave it into the fabric of your situation."

"If you always strive for improvement, then you always have something to look forward to."

"When you have dealt with so much bullshyt your perception is altered to think everyone's stuff will turn into crap."

"Just because you love someone doesn't mean you have to be stupid."

"Never be afraid to wear your flaws for everyone to see. It is not a sign of weakness but rather shows exactly how strong you are and what you have been through. It may inspire someone who is having difficulty to do the same."

"Authenticity is such a rarity these days that some women mistake it for diamonds and men mistake it for cufflinks. Authenticity is to be worn at all times and not for those occasions that you deem special."

"Sometimes people act up because they have difficulty keeping up."

"When you hurt others you lose a bit of yourself that cannot be retrieved."

"People follow trends when they are missing that creative thought to create something that springs from originality."

"What you say with your mouth is not as powerful as what you say in your mind."

"The biggest mirrors in your life will show you the potential of your greatest reflection."

"Let your actions be bigger than the words that leave your lips."

"Silence can be your best friend if you know to utilize it correctly."

"Always be inspired to do the right thing for yourself regardless of what others think."

"One of the best moments of clarity is when you finish crying."

"One simple truth can destroy the greatest lie ever told."

"You never truly understand someone until you have hurt them in such a way that years later it comes back to haunt your current mind set ."

"Compliancy will get you nowhere and you will remain static."

"Some are impressed by the meager things and others are inspired to do and gain great things."

"The answers that you seek are in front of you. You just haven't realized it yet."

"If you can't keep a promise to yourself, how are you able to keep a promise to others?"

"Sometimes it takes a little bit of courage to do something extraordinarily big."

"Never lose sight of the things worth fighting for. If you didn't want it so badly it would be easy. Keep fighting!"

"When things are the most complicated it only means a great blessing is awaiting you. Do not get stuck in the mundane!"

"Some people have a warped sense of security that will never be real."

"Idolize the spiritual connection and not the material."

"True happiness consists of three things: mind, body, and soul. Happiness in the mind allows you to experience a euphoric feeling that is vibrated, and then happiness in the body is known. Yet happiness in the soul is fermented longer because the inner man has a strong hold on it. Balance of all three is critical to true happiness."

"Unless you have a better solution to living life, it is best to stick with that you know from the experiences you have had. Never judge another person's method for living their life by your own ideologies."

"Some people lack the ability to see how much of a change needs to occur because of the negative repetitiveness that is surrounding them. Reality will never settle in for those who wish to keep sleeping in a dream-like state."

"Refuse to be anything ordinary and determine to be even more extraordinary."

"Negative traffic in your mind creates daily jams in your flow of actions toward others. Time to create a detour!"

"Only a fool is sure of themselves in a unsure situation."

"Some need to learn how to speak to another person's spirit rather than listen to the lust that comes out."

"Some people will dislike you for how much you believe in yourself. Keep believing in you!"

"When people hurt others it goes to show the level of pain they are in."

"Never let outer beauty be stronger than your inner beauty."

"Be concerned and care for others but never worry about them."

"Discernment can be a key component in finding a logical answer to a peculiar question."

"Some things are worth the value and other things are not worth the flesh they come wrapped up in. Know the difference in what you see and feel."

"Some people's standards are so low that they are starting to favor dust on the ground."

"You will never fully appreciate the quality of a person until you understand the quantity of the things they been through."

"Decide how you want to share your light, your type of sunshine. Will your light help someone ignite their spark or will you shield it from the world?"

"Doing better doesn't mean obtaining earthly possessions but doing those things that make your soul rise and treating others more humanely."

"A certain amount of pain is needed to push us to our next level of existence."

"There is no substitution for doing the right thing when the right thing needs to be done."

"We all want something that is real and tangible, but some are not willing to wait for it."

"Admire those who have wisdom because you are learning the viability of a priceless experience."

"There is no substitution for happiness. It is within your reach and all you have to do is grab it and never let go."

"No one can teach you how to be a leader; it comes from within."

"When you're comfortable in your own skin everything else becomes secondary."

"Never allow yourself to be the subject in the negative sentence, but instead be the positive period at the end."

"Never give someone the feeling of false hope. Don't tell them you love them if you don't mean it, don't say that you care and fail to show it, and don't say things just because they sound good. Everyone deserves a level of honesty that builds trust. Once that trust is broken you never truly get it back 100%."

"Silence is not the equivalent of being angry, not wanting to be heard, or not caring. Lots of positive things occur in silence…peace happens in silence, words are interpreted in a different way, and there is also much inward and outward caring that is expressed."

"There is more to 'growing up' than just the physicality of it. If you are not able to fully comprehend growing up in a mental, emotional, and spiritual state, then you are just a child dressed in your parents' clothing, pretending to be a 'grownup.' Lack of communication translates to 'playing games,' and that right there is something a child does."

"In that moment when you realize the epiphany your soul gives you and tells you where 'home' truly is, have enough common sense to 'come home.' It wants to dwell in that place of peace, love, happiness, and laughter."

"Just because you are not accustomed to something good does not mean you shouldn't have it. Get accustomed to it, because it has been presented to you for a reason."

"Some things are better comprehended not by talking but by doing."

"Everyone has a certain fire in their eyes, but the question is, are they able to handle the intensity of the heat contained within?"

"When someone can see what your mess is with clarity, then you should realize it is not as bad as you might think."

"The only requirement in finding yourself is to be real with yourself."
"Be so busy with entertaining what you will become that you do not have the time to entertain foolishness."

"Once you discover your reason there will be no need for options."

"Never be satisfied with the mundane when you were born to be epic."

"Some people have difficulty speaking the truth because their mouth is full of shyt."

"There is a difference between priorities and mind games. One will gain your respect, honesty, and loyalty, whereas with the other one you will lose things of quality."

"Find friends who will elevate you to your greatest potential."

"You should be past the age where mind games are relevant."

"Bullshyt sells more quickly than the truth. More people need to be subscribers to the truth and throw out the false reality that comes with dealing bullshyt."

"You cannot do simple math with those who refuse to cancel out the inconsistent variables."

"You should crave something that this world can never give you and something you just cannot live without."

"Crave the necessities and block out the impurities."

"A true and pure heart is the best thing to have when you are struggling with toxic situations."

"You must be loyal to yourself first before you can be loyal to others."

"Those who crave the simple things have to be willing to become what has already been placed in you."

"Telling the truth will either set things straight or set things off."

"Instead of mimicking another's pain and then displaying it for the world to see, try to understand it and end the cycle. Become more than a domino of pain; be the healer."

"A moment of clarity is more awakening than hours of overthinking."

"So many things can be solved if we allowed ourselves to become unstuck."

"Those things that can be accounted for still have the ability to go missing, and when they do they will never add up properly."

"If you lack the ability to communicate, then your words unspoken will never have meaning."

"Sometimes your own validation will come from your own intuition."

"Once you understand your uniqueness, no one can box you in."

"People may remove the mask, but they cannot remove what is hidden in the eyes."

"The world is going to laugh at you but you have to learn when and how to laugh at the world."

"Be on a level where BS cannot exist and time won't be wasted."

"The realest things you possess is your heart and mind."

"Adaptability comes when you learn to live without human limitations that you create."

"If you continue to behave in foolish ways, instead of being A fool you become THE fool."

"Some people should be treated either as a multiple-choice or a fill-in-the-blank."

"Some will create a statement while others will create a question."

"People can kill something so beautiful because of the recreation of setbacks playing out in their minds."

"Sometimes you cannot be present for another's own elevation."

"A woman cannot speak life into her man if he continuously wants to play dead in different situations."

"A mind full of doubt will never understand a heart full of hope."

"You cannot have an eagle mentality with pigeon tendencies. Certain things are just not going to fly right."

"You could paint the ideal image for someone and they would still reach the conclusion that it is the equivalent of a blank canvas, a waterless cup, and a dry-ass brush."

"The only thing that plays games is the ego. The spirit does not play games because it only knows love. Remove the ego, find the spirit, and embrace love."

"Some people are not meant to understand or even get 'your hustle,' and you know why? Because your hustle is for you and they should find the means to get their own."

"Your soul is so deep that in order for someone to truly know you, hand them a shovel and tell them to start digging."

"Those who desire the simple things in life find happiness in all the little things and smile for no reason."

"Every situation requires a different type of glove to be used in order to be handled correctly. You cannot handle adult situations with kiddie gloves."

"No matter the size, shape, or form, a blessing is still a blessing. So when you receive it, be careful how you treat it."

"Mind your own frequency and see where you end up at."

"Sometimes you have rare moments and if you are really aware you can get insight in plain sight."

"If you are caught looking up too high or looking down too low, you can miss the blessing that is coming toward you at eye level. Focus on the blessing that is coming forward."

"Quick fixes only bring temporary happiness. Why would you want temporary when happiness is suppose to be long-lasting?"

"Dead weights cannot hang around those who are meant to be balloons and fly."

"There is a big difference between hearing and listening. Don't just hear for the sake of hearing but fully participate in the beautification of listening to what is being said."

"Just because it can become cold outside does not mean you have to be bitter on the inside. Forgiveness is best felt when you learn how to warm up your own heart, and it will flow to the better parts of you."

"If you learn to be loyal in the smallest things, then when it comes to the large things it will be so simple."

"You should want to mingle with those individuals who bring a tsunami of positive change rather than to mingle with those who find comfort in playing in a puddle of static water."

"It is easy to want to be something else or someone else, but the real power is to always be yourself when other forces try to take over. It takes courage to be you and nobody can do for you but you."

"The person you were yesterday is gone, the person ready for today is here, and the person you will become tomorrow has not arrived yet, but what you can do is prepare for it with a smile."

# About The Author

Ms. Seleta Harvey has a background in architecture and interior design, but her love of art and writing was instilled in her as a child and has progressed since then. She has studied at Howard Community College, New York Institute of Technology, and the Art Institute of Pittsburgh – Online Division. She is currently working full-time and running her own art business, called Pure Vision Art Co., and goes by the name of 4everguardedartist. Her first published work was a poem titled "Closer" many years ago in a collection with other fellow poets. She now resides in Maryland, where she continues to focus on writing and creating abstract art. Her personal interests include sports, fitness, food, traveling, being a nature lover, spending time with family and friends, inspirational blogging, and going anywhere life takes her.

Websites:
www.purevisionartco.wix.com/4everguardedartist
Instagram: 4everguardedartist

www.ingramcontent.com/pod-product-compliance
Lightning Source LLC
Chambersburg PA
CBHW070115080526
44586CB00013B/1297